42 Vegan Protein Shakes and Smoothies

Quick, Easy and Perfect for Clean Eating

I

Kelli Rae

42 Vegan Protein Shakes and Smoothies: Quick, Easy and
Perfect for Clean Eating

The information provided in this book is designed to provide
helpful information on the subjects discussed. This book is not
meant to be used, nor should it be used, to diagnose or treat any
medical condition. For diagnosis or treatment of any medical
problem, consult your own physician. The publisher and author
are not responsible for any specific health or allergy needs that
may require medical supervision and are not liable for any
damages or negative consequences from any treatment, action,
application or preparation, to any person reading or following the
information in this book.

Table of Contents

ATTENTION: Get Your Free Gift <u>HERE</u>!

Do you have a big sweet tooth? Are you looking for a solution to "cure" your sweet tooth, but still be healthy?

What I have done is put together 6 of my favorite healthy, yet sinfully sweet snacks. They are super simple to make and I wanted to share them with YOU!

It's my simple way of saying THANK YOU for downloading this book. Go to <u>http://free.kelliraefit.com</u> NOW to download!

Kelli Rae

Introduction

Smoothies are delicious and have so many health benefits. They provide great nutrition, and can be a great cure for a "sweet tooth". They are quick, easy to make, and you can make them for any meal or snack of the day.

In this recipe book, I have included 42 vegan smoothies and protein shakes that are easy and quick to make. I have also included my top five tips and tricks for smoothies, as well as a quick and fun fact about an ingredient with each recipe.

Please be advised that I am not a nutritionist and if you need to make a substitution of an ingredient, please do that. You will know your body better than me. These are just some of my favorites and suggestions to try. These recipes are NOT medical advice.

All of these smoothies make 1 to 2, just depending on how hungry you are.

I hope you enjoy this collection of recipes! If you have any suggestions or questions, you can always send me an email at kelliraefit@gmail.com or follow me on Instagram @kelliraefit.

Top 5 Tips and Tricks

~ Ice is great when you want to make a smoothie thicker. But to get the best consistency, about ⅔ of your ingredients should be frozen. This is just a general guide as it will depend on your blender.

~ No time to make smoothies when you want? No problem! Prepare them ahead of time and place the ingredients in a Ziploc bag. Place the bags in the fridge or freezer and grab them as needed.

~ To avoid leafy chunks in green smoothies, make sure to blend your leafy greens and liquids first. Then add the remaining ingredients.

~ Ran out of ice? All of your ingredients are fresh instead of frozen? BUT you still want a thick shake? No problem! Just add less liquids. Start with half the recommended amount, and you can always add more if needed.

~ If you have a little bit of extra smoothie, pour it into an ice cube tray or small paper cups. Freeze and enjoy later as a special treat.

Chia Berry Smoothie

Chia seeds are very high in antioxidants. However if you are on high blood pressure or blood thinner medications, check with your doctor before consuming them.

Ingredients
1 cup unsweetened vanilla almond milk
1/2 cup blueberries, frozen
1/4 cup cherries, frozen
1 Tbsp Chia seeds

Directions
1 - Put the almond milk in the blender.
2 - Add the rest of the ingredients.
3 - Mix until blended and smooth.

ENJOY!

Strawberry Banana-tastic Smoothie

This is a classic smoothie using strawberries, bananas and almond milk.

Ingredients
2 cups strawberries
1 banana
1 cup unsweetened almond milk
Ice (optional for thickness)

Directions
1 - Put the almond milk in the blender.
2 - Add the rest of the ingredients.
3 - Mix until blended and smooth.

ENJOY!

Perfectly Green Nutty Smoothie

Even though almonds are high in fat content, they can help with
weight loss.

Ingredients
8-10 natural, raw almonds
2-3 strawberries
1 banana
1 to 1 1/2 cup water (for preferred thickness)
1/2 cup kale
1/2 cup spinach
1/2 cup avocado

Directions
1 - Pour 1/2 cup of water and the kale in the blender.
2 - Add the remaining ingredients, except the rest of the water.
3 - Mix until blended.
4 - If the smoothie is too thick for you, add a little more water
and mix.
5 - Repeat if necessary.

ENJOY!

Easy Tropical Pineapple Smoothie

Did you know that fresh spinach is low in calories, but pretty high in protein?

Ingredients
2 cups fresh pineapple, chopped
1 cup fresh spinach
1 cup light coconut milk

Directions
1 - Put the coconut milk and the spinach in the blender.
2 - Mix together, then add the pineapple.
3 - Mix until blended and smooth.

ENJOY!

Watermelon Coconut Tropical Smoothie

Watermelon has a very high level of lycopene. This has been proven to help with heart and bone health, as well as aid in the prevention of prostate cancer.

Ingredients
2 cups seedless watermelon
1 cup strawberries
1 cup almond coconut milk
Ice (add as needed for thickness)

Directions
1 - Put the almond milk in the blender.
2 - Add the watermelon and strawberries.
3 - Mix until blended and smooth.
4 - If smoothie is too thin, add a few ice cubes. Mix until smooth. Repeat if needed if you would like a thicker smoothie.

ENJOY!

"Get Yo Protein" Yummy Shake

Strawberries are a very good source of vitamin C. Just 1/2 cup provides 50% of the daily recommended value.

Ingredients
1 medium banana
1 scoop vegan protein powder
½ cup strawberries
½ cup blueberries
1 cup unsweetened vanilla almond milk

Directions
1 - Put the almond milk in the blender.
2 - Add the rest of the ingredients.
2 - Mix until blended and smooth.

ENJOY!

Tropical Tango Smoothie

Almond non-dairy yogurt is very creamy and a good source of fiber.

Ingredients
1 medium orange, peeled and chopped
1 mango, peeled and chopped
1 cup vanilla almond non-dairy yogurt
1 cup strawberries
Water (optional)

Directions
1 - Add all ingredients to your blender.
2 - Mix until blended and smooth.
3 - If smoothie is too thick for you, add some water slowly and mix.

ENJOY!

The Green Quickness Smoothie

Kale is a low calorie food and has many nutritional benefits.

Ingredients
1 medium banana
1 small avocado, peeled and pit removed, chopped
1 small Granny Smith apple, chopped
1 cup kale, chopped
1 cup original unsweetened almond milk
Ice (add as needed for thickness)

Directions
1 - Put the almond milk and kale in the blender. Mix.
2 - Add the rest of the ingredients.
3 - Mix until blended and smooth.
4 - If smoothie is too thin, add a few ice cubes. Mix until smooth.
Repeat if needed if you would like a thicker smoothie.

ENJOY!

The Green Monster Hulk Smoothie

Due to it's fiber and protein content, peanut butter can help you
in your weight loss journey. It keeps you fuller longer and helps
fight cravings.

Ingredients
2 handfuls of spinach
1 medium banana
1 scoop vegan protein powder
1 cup unsweetened almond milk
1 Tbsp Chia seeds
1 Tbsp natural peanut butter

Directions
1 - Put the almond milk and spinach in the blender. Mix.
2 - Add the rest of the ingredients.
3 - Mix until blended and smooth.

ENJOY!

The Healthy Cocktail Green Smoothie

A lime is used in many different products, and it has a long list of health benefits.

Ingredients
1 1/2 cups fresh pineapple, chopped
1 cup kale, chopped
1 cup coconut water
1 lime, juiced

Directions
1 - Put the coconut water and kale in the blender and mix.
2 - Add the remaining ingredients.
3 - Mix until blended and smooth.

ENJOY!

"Quit Monkeying Around" PB Smoothie

An 8-ounce glass of hemp milk contains all 10 essential amino acids.

<u>Ingredients</u>
2 small frozen bananas, sliced
4 small dates, pitted and chopped
1/2 cup hemp milk
1 Tbsp natural peanut butter
1 Tbsp Chia seeds
Water (depending on preferred thickness)

<u>Directions</u>
1 - Put the hemp milk in the blender.
2 - Add the rest of the ingredients to your blender, except for the water.
3 - Mix until blended and smooth.
4 - If this is too thick for you, add some water and mix until blended.

ENJOY!

Strawberry Mint Creamy Smoothie

Spearmint has many different uses, including aiding in digestive disorders.

Ingredients
1/2 medium banana, frozen
1/2 medium avocado
2 cups fresh strawberries
1 1/2 cups coconut water
3 Tbsp spearmint extract
1 pitted date (optional)
Ice (optional for thickness)

Directions
1 - Put the coconut water in the blender.
2 - Add the rest of the ingredients, except for the ice.
3 - Mix until blended and smooth.
4 - If this is too thin for you, add some ice and mix until blended.
If it is still too thin, repeat until it's to your preferred thickness.

ENJOY!

Amazing Chocolate-y Banana Buffness Shake

It can be difficult to find a vegan protein powder that tastes good. My favorite is by Raw Fusion. It mixes very well and tastes pretty good.

Ingredients
1 scoop chocolate vegan protein powder
1 medium banana
1 cup unsweetened chocolate almond milk
1 Tbsp unsweetened baking cocoa
3-5 ice cubes (add as needed for thickness)

Directions
1 - Put the almond milk in the blender.
2 - Add the rest of ingredients, except for the ice.
3 - Mix until blended and smooth.
4 - If this is too thin for you, add some ice and mix until blended. Add more ice and mix again if necessary.

ENJOY!

Berry Banana-Iwi Smoothie

Pomegranate has many different health and beauty benefits.

Ingredients
2 kiwis, peeled
2 small bananas, peeled
1 1/2 cups whole strawberries
1 cup blueberries
3/4 cup pomegranate seeds

Directions
1 - Add all ingredients to your blender.
2 - Mix until blended and smooth.

ENJOY!

Simple Colada Delight Smoothie

Even though coconut milk has a higher level of saturated fat, it still has many health benefits, including the aid of weight loss.

Ingredients
1 medium banana, sliced
1 cup fresh pineapple, chopped
1 cup coconut milk

Directions
1 - Put the coconut milk in the blender.
2 - Add the banana and pineapple.
3 - Mix until blended and smooth.

ENJOY!

Super Duper Blueberry Smoothie

Kale has more calcium than milk and more vitamin C than an orange.

Ingredients
4 leaves of kale, chopped
1 medium banana, peeled and frozen
1/2 cup blueberries, frozen
1/2 cup orange juice
2 Tbsp ground flax seeds

Directions
1 - Put the orange juice and kale in the blender.
2 - Add the rest of the ingredients.
3 - Mix until blended and smooth.

ENJOY!

Refreshingly Awesome Cherry Smoothie

Do you have any bananas that have too many brown spots? Try
peeling and freezing them for a healthy snack!

Ingredients
1 medium banana, sliced and frozen
1 cup cherries, frozen
1/2 cup coconut water
1/2 tsp vanilla extract
1 packet Stevia (if needed for taste)

Directions
1 - Put the coconut water in the blender.
2 - Add the rest of the ingredients.
3 - Mix until blended and smooth.

ENJOY!

Detoxifying Yummy Green Smoothie

If you don't have baby spinach, you can always substitute regular spinach. It's essentially the same, but baby spinach was harvested much earlier in the plant's life.

Ingredients
1 medium banana, chopped and frozen
1 medium pear, chopped
1 1/2 cups orange juice
1 cup baby spinach
1 cup kale, chopped

Directions
1 - Put the orange juice and kale in the blender.
2 - Add the rest of the ingredients.
3 - Mix until blended and smooth.

ENJOY!

Chocolate Nutty Vegan Smoothie

Sunbutter is made from sunflower seeds, and it's a good nut butter alternative.

Ingredients
2 dates, chopped
1/3 cup chopped cauliflower
1/2 cup unsweetened vanilla almond milk
2 Tbsp Sunbutter
2 Tbsp Vegan dark chocolate
Raw hemp hearts for a garnish
1/2 cup ice (add as needed for thickness)

Directions
1 - Put the almond milk in the blender.
2 - Add the rest of the ingredients, except for the ice.
3 - Mix until blended and smooth.
4 - If this is too thin for you, add some ice and mix until blended.
Repeat if necessary to your preferred thickness.

ENJOY!

The Blueberry Bomb Protein Shake

Psyllium husk is a small seed found in the bulk food section.

Ingredients
1 medium banana
1 scoop of vanilla soy protein
1 cup unsweetened vanilla almond milk
1/2 cup of frozen blueberries
1/2 Tbsp of flax seed oil
1 tsp psyllium husk

Directions
1 - Put the almond milk in the blender.
2 - Add the rest of the ingredients.
3 - Mix until blended and smooth.

ENJOY!

Fruitie Greenie Smoothie

Granny Smith apples have a higher acid content than other
apples, so they won't go brown as fast once you cut into them.

<u>Ingredients</u>
2 cups of honeydew, chopped
1 Granny Smith apple, chopped
1 kiwi, peeled and chopped
1 Tbsp lemon juice
1 cup ice cubes (add as needed for thickness)

<u>Directions</u>
1 - Put all ingredients in the blender, except for the ice.
2 - Mix until blended and smooth.
3 - If this is too thin for you, add some ice and mix until blended.
Repeat if necessary if you prefer a thicker smoothie.

ENJOY!

Delicious Green Smoothie

A cucumber is a great food anytime, but especially during the summer months as it's composed of important electrolytes and water.

Ingredients
2 kiwis, peeled and chopped
1 medium banana, chopped
1 handful of fresh spinach
1/2 cup cucumber, chopped
Ice (as needed for thickness)

Directions
1 - Add all of the ingredients to your blender.
2 - Mix until blended and smooth.
3 - If this is too thin for you, add some ice and mix until blended.

ENJOY!

Marvelously Fruity Cleansing Smoothie

Need a healthy snack idea? Try freezing grapes - a perfect treat for a hot summer day!

<u>Ingredients</u>
15 green grapes
6 strawberries
2 large handfuls of spinach
2 slices of raw red beet, chopped
1 scoop vegan protein powder
1 cup water
½ cucumber, skin removed
½ orange, peeled
4-6 ice cubes (add as needed for thickness)

<u>Directions</u>
1 - Put the water in the blender.
2 - Add the rest of the ingredients, except for the ice.
3 - Mix until blended and smooth.
4 - If this is too thin for you, add some ice and mix until blended.

ENJOY!

Banana Nut Spice Smoothie

Coconut butter has many health benefits, including aiding anxiety and supporting the thyroid.

Ingredients
2 medjool dates, pitted
1 medium banana
1 cup unsweetened almond milk
1 tsp coconut butter
½ tsp chai spice
Ice (if needed for thickness)

Directions
1 - Put the almond milk in the blender.
2 - Add the rest of the ingredients.
3 - Mix until blended and smooth.

ENJOY!

Cherry Covered Protein Smoothie

A cup of chocolate almond milk has about the same amount of sugar as Coca-Cola. Therefore, it is best to look for unsweetened varieties.

<u>Ingredients</u>
1 cup unsweetened almond milk
1 cup pitted cherries, fresh or frozen
1 scoop vegan protein powder
2 tsp almond butter
1 tsp pure almond extract
6-8 ice cubes (add as needed for thickness)

<u>Directions</u>
1 - Put the almond milk in the blender.
2 - Add the rest of the ingredients, except for the ice.
3 - Mix until blended and smooth.
4 - If this is too thin for you, add some ice and mix until blended.

ENJOY!

Mouth Watering Strawberry Cheesecake Smoothie

The cashew is not really a nut. It's actually a seed.

<u>Ingredients</u>
1 cup strawberries
1 cup unsweetened vanilla almond milk
½ lemon, peeled
1 Tbsp cashew butter
Ice (if needed for thickness)

<u>Directions</u>
1 - Put the almond milk in the blender.
2 - Add the rest of the ingredients.
3 - Mix until blended and smooth.
4 - If this is too thin for you, add some ice and mix until blended.

ENJOY!

Perfectly Poppy Raspberry Smoothie

Poppy seeds can cause a false positive drug test. However, the
levels are not high enough to cause an addiction.

Ingredients
1 cup unsweetened almond milk
1 cup raspberries
1 Tbsp lemon juice
1 Tbsp almond butter
1 Tbsp Chia seeds
1 1/2 tsp poppy seeds
Ice (if needed for thickness)

Directions
1 - Put the almond milk in the blender.
2 - Add the rest of the ingredients.
3 - Mix until blended and smooth.
4 - If this is too thin for you, add some ice and mix until blended.

ENJOY!

Spicy Lime Mango Protein Smoothie

Spiciness of a jalapeno can depend on when it was cultivated and the method of preparation. Not all jalapenos are the same.

Ingredients
1 small banana
1/2 lime, peeled
1/2 avocado
3/4 cup frozen mango
1 Tbsp jalepeño, chopped
1 cup unsweetened almond milk

Directions
1 - Put the almond milk in the blender.
2 - Add the rest of the ingredients.
3 - Mix until blended and smooth.

ENJOY

Cinnamon Berry Blast Protein Smoothie

Cinnamon has a numerous amount of health benefits. Among these are lowering blood sugar levels and reducing factors for heart disease.

Ingredients
1 scoop vegan protein powder
1 small banana, frozen
1 cup unsweetened almond milk
3/4 cup cherries, frozen
2 tsp cinnamon
3-4 ice cubes (add as needed for thickness)

Directions
1 - Put the almond milk in the blender.
2 - Add the rest of the ingredients.
3 - Mix until blended and smooth.
4 - If this is too thin for you, add some ice and mix until blended.

ENJOY!

Basically Sweet Berry Smoothie

There are over 200 different species of raspberries around the world.

Ingredients
1 medium banana
3/4 cup orange juice
1 cup strawberries, frozen
1 cup raspberries, frozen

Directions
1 - Put the orange juice in the blender.
2 - Add the rest of the ingredients.
3 - Mix until blended and smooth.

ENJOY!

Luscious Mango Berry Smoothie

Many processed foods that are blueberry flavored don't even
have real blueberries in them.

Ingredients
5 large strawberries
2 medium bananas
1 mango
1 handful blueberries
1/2 cup unsweetened vanilla almond milk

Directions
1 - Put the almond milk in the blender.
2 - Add the rest of the ingredients.
3 - Mix until blended and smooth.

ENJOY!

The Tropics Smoothie

Mangoes are very popular. In India, baskets of mangoes are considered signs of friendship.

Ingredients
1 medium banana
1 cup mango, frozen
1 cup coconut milk
1 Tbsp ground flax seed

Directions
1 - Put the coconut milk in the blender.
2 - Add the rest of the ingredients.
3 - Mix until blended and smooth.

ENJOY!

Melon Ball Beach Smoothie

The peach was originated in China. It is considered to be a symbol of immortality and unity.

Ingredients
1 medium banana
2 pitted dates, chopped
1 cup watermelon, chopped
1/2 cup peach, sliced
3-5 ice cubes (add as needed for thickness)

Directions
1 - Add all of the ingredients to your blender, except for the ice.
2 - Mix until blended and smooth.
3 - If this is too thin for you, add some ice and mix until blended.

ENJOY!

Sparkly Sour Citrus Smoothie

Lemon juice has many different benefits. One of these is hair care, as it helps dandruff and can give hair extra shine.

<u>Ingredients</u>
1 medium banana
1/2 cup water
1/4 cup orange juice
3 Tbsp lemon juice
2 Tbsp lime juice
3 ice cubes (add as needed for thickness)

<u>Directions</u>
1 - Put the water and orange juice in the blender.
2 - Add the rest of the ingredients, except for the ice.
3 - Mix until blended and smooth.
4 - If this is too thin for you, add some ice and mix until blended.

ENJOY!

Chocolaty Nut Butter Smoothie

Stevia is becoming more popular and it's a good substitute for
artificial sweeteners, like Splenda.

<u>Ingredients</u>
1 small banana, peeled
1/4 cup baby spinach
1/4 cup unsweetened almond milk
1/2 Tbsp cocoa
1/2 Tbsp almond butter
1 pack of Stevia
3 ice cubes (add as needed for thickness)

<u>Directions</u>
1 - Put the almond milk and baby spinach in the blender.
2 - Add the rest of the ingredients, except for the ice.
3 - Mix until blended and smooth.
4 - If this is too thin for you, add some ice and mix until blended.
Repeat if necessary.

ENJOY!

Melon Banana Smoothie

Honeydew melon is typically green. However, it can also be orange and this is called temptation melon.

Ingredients
1 medium banana
1 pitted date, chopped
1 cup honeydew, chopped
1/2 cup cantaloupe, chopped
1/4 cup water

Directions
1 - Put the water in the blender.
2 - Add the rest of the ingredients.
3 - Mix until blended and smooth.

ENJOY!

Green Sunrise Smoothie

Frozen pineapple is a great snack to help with sweet cravings.

Ingredients
1 small banana, frozen
1 cup baby spinach
1/2 cup unsweetened almond milk
1/4 cup pineapple, frozen
1 Tbsp ground flax seed

Directions
1 - Put the almond milk and baby spinach in the blender.
2 - Add the rest of the ingredients.
3 - Mix until blended and smooth.

ENJOY!

Tropical Acai Smoothie

The acai berry is considered a superfood. However, there is still limited research and there are claims about health benefits haven't been 100% proven.

Ingredients
1 small banana, frozen
3/4 cup mango, chopped
1/2 cup unsweetened coconut milk
1/2 cup acai juice
1/4 cup baby spinach
2-3 ice cubes (add as needed for thickness)

Directions
1 - Put the coconut milk, acai juice and baby spinach in the blender. Mix briefly.
2 - Add the rest of the ingredients, except for the ice.
3 - Mix until blended and smooth.
4 - If this is too thin for you, add some ice and mix until blended. Repeat if necessary.

ENJOY!

Cantaloupe Crusher Smoothie

Iceberg lettuce is 96 percent water!

Ingredients
1 medium banana, peeled and sliced
1 cup cantaloupe, chopped
1/2 cup unsweetened almond milk
1/2 cup iceberg lettuce
1/2 cup ice (add as needed for thickness)

Directions
1 - Put the almond milk and iceberg lettuce in the blender.
2 - Add the rest of the ingredients, except for the ice.
3 - Mix until blended and smooth.
4 - If this is too thin for you, add some ice and mix until blended.
Repeat if necessary.

ENJOY!

Delightfully Delicious Apple Smoothie

There are many different types of red apples. In this recipe, pick your favorite variety!

Ingredients
1 red apple, chopped
1 1/2 cups natural apple juice
1/2 cup cherries, pitted
1 cup ice (add as needed for thickness)

Directions
1 - Put the apple juice in the blender.
2 - Add the rest of the ingredients, except for the ice.
3 - Mix until blended and smooth.
4 - If this is too thin for you, add some ice and mix until blended. Repeat if necessary.

ENJOY!

Berry Cream Smoothie

There are over 500 varieties of avocados in the entire world.

<u>Ingredients</u>
1/4 medium avocado
1 1/2 cups coconut water
1/2 cup mixed berries, frozen
1 Tbsp unsweetened shredded coconut
1 tsp spirulina

<u>Directions</u>
1 - Put the coconut water in the blender.
2 - Add the rest of the ingredients.
3 - Mix until blended and smooth.

ENJOY!

Chocolate Banana Nutty Smoothie

Most Americans do not get enough potassium in their diets, and coconut water can help fill these gaps.

Ingredients
1 medium banana, frozen
1 cup coconut water
2 Tbsp cashews
2 Tbsp hulled hemp seed
1 Tbsp unsweetened cocoa powder
1/2 cup ice (add as needed for thickness)

Directions
1 - Put the coconut water in the blender.
2 - Add the rest of the ingredients, except for the ice.
3 - Mix until blended and smooth.
4 - If this is too thin for you, add some ice and mix until blended. Repeat if necessary.

ENJOY!

ABOUT THE AUTHOR

Kelli Rae is a vegan and has been involved with the health and fitness industry for most of her life. She has played many competitive sports, from softball, to volleyball and tennis. She has also competed in two bikini competitions. She loves helping other people achieve their goals, and currently lives in Arizona with her husband Dale and rescue cat Izzie.

Printed in Great Britain
by Amazon